The Legacy

SALLY GUISE

A light hearted account of life in an English country house in the late 1900s and early 2000s, where the Guise family (one of the oldest families in England) lived – deeply committed to their local community. . . and probably the last time the house will ever be used as a family home.

Sally Guise 1935 -2016

A country girl at heart, Sally grew up in post war Malvern, Worcestershire and Frampton-on-Severn, Gloucestershire; she enjoyed being an active member of the local pony club and a keen follower of Croome Hunt. Sally lived most of her working life in London sustained by regular visits to the countryside to see family and friends. Marrying Sir John Guise and moving to Elmore, she felt she had returned to her roots.

Sally was passionately keen to write about her life at Elmore, where, with her husband John, she shared with him and the local community a lifestyle steeped in history, but one which was perhaps unlikely to last. Sally felt that writing about it would provide a record for later generations as well as a vote of thanks to those with whom her experiences had been shared, in what was becoming a rapidly changing world.

The contents of this book are Sally to the core, as those who knew her will appreciate. During the last two years of her life, as Sally worked to complete this book, she knew that she was suffering from a terminal illness. She managed to complete very largely what she set out to do. With the help of the team Sally already had in place, it has been a privilege to finally complete her vision and publish this book.

Bill, Kate and David Stevens   May 2017

Sally was grateful to the many people who helped her prepare this book for publication. In particular Rosie Daniels for all her typing, the people who painstakingly checked each chapter and Nick and Tom Allen for putting the text and photographs together so beautifully for John Chandler to publish.

The photographs are largely taken by Sally and are from her personal albums. Grateful thanks is given to the professional photographers who have kindly given their permission for their work to be included: Carol Ann Johnson, John Wigan and bjphotography.

Contents

This is the story of my married life spent at Elmore Court
– the Guise family home in Gloucestershire,
the enormous interest, hard work, love and pleasure that it brought;
deep fulfilment, wonderful friends and a life full of purpose.

And the prayer that inspired me . . .
GOD grant me the serenity to accept the things I cannot change ;
the courage to change the things I can; and the wisdom to know the difference.

Genealogy

The Guises are of Norman extraction, originally de Gyes, and were Lords of St. Valery a small coastal town in the north of France. They came to England with William the Conqueror and first settled at Apsley Guise in Bedfordshire. Elmore came into the family in 1262 as part of the dowry of the bride of Nicolas de Gyse. It has been a family home ever since.

The family later exchanged their property at Apsley Guise for Brockworth in Gloucestershire and thereafter bought further properties at Rendcombe and Highnam. However, eventually all of these were sold and Elmore became the family's headquarters – which it has remained.

THE BARONETS OF ELMORE

The Baronetcy of Elmore was created in 1661 – possibly in appreciation of the family's strong support for the Royalist cause during the Civil War. Christopher Guise became the 1st Baronet of Elmore and it is thought that it was at about this time that the family bought the manor and estates of Rendcombe from the Berkeleys. This was for a while their chief residence. However, on the death of the 5th Baronet of Elmore, William Guise (1737-1783), the Baronetcy became extinct.

THE BARONETS OF HIGHNAM

Shortly after the death of the 5th Baronet of Elmore, his cousin John was created 1st Baronet of Highnam and was subsequently succeeded by each of his two sons. It was the younger of these two sons – John Wright (1777-1865) –who eventually sold the estates of Highnam, Rendcombe and Brockworth and the family returned to Elmore which became their sole residence.

A particularly admirable man and a brilliant soldier, Sir John Wright Guise, 3rd Baronet of Highnam, rose to become a senior general in the British army. He fought in the Peninsula War with the Duke of Wellington and was honoured with the Grand Cross of the Order of Bath for gallantry. He was granted the privilege of bearing supporters to his heraldic arms. He is buried in Gloucester Cathedral.

My husband, Sir John Grant Guise, 7th Baronet of Highnam, spent most of his life at Elmore. As a child he was brought up there and apart from a brief spell during the Second World War when the government commandeered the house and the Guise family moved to Scotland, he was based at Elmore for his entire life. He was educated at Winchester and Sandhurst and had a ten-year army career in the 3rd Hussars before becoming a starter for the Jockey Club – a job he loved – for twenty five years.

Margaret Guise, his mother, married Sir Anselm Guise (1888-1970), 6th Baronet of Highnam when she was twenty-four. She lived until she was ninety-four. A highly respected and much loved member of Elmore community, she involved herself in every aspect of village life. Before her marriage she was Margaret Grant. The Grants were Scots and her father, James Augustus, was M.P. for Cumberland and later made a Baronet. He was the son of James Augustus Grant the African explorer who, with Speke, discovered the source of the Nile.

1.

The Caravanners

At the age of seventy – and recently widowed – Margaret Guise bought a caravan and attached it to the back of her ageing Rover car. She felt that during her married life, she had not seen enough of the world – and began to plan the first of what was to become many overseas trips with her friends. My mother Romie Stevens was one of them.

Each trip involved a great deal of planning – and some hilarious lunch parties took place where these plans were laid. I can remember being at home for at least one of them and the plans were original, to say the least.

Margaret took three of her friends on each of the overseas trips; two slept in the caravan and two in the car. The friends varied slightly and were not always the same four and the trips lasted for as long as it took. The destinations were France, Switzerland, Italy, Greece and Romania, to name but a few. Resources were pooled and kept in a velvet drawstring bag. Before leaving they were each expected to have mustered a variety of rather unusual things. At the pre-trip lunch party that I remember – the list amused me for its originality. Everything was extremely practical – but so was the group going on holiday. Wellington boots, a ball of string, a bucket, a torch. These were some of the essentials to be taken. Then there was the list of food. Tins of ham etc.

The trip was a frugal affair – but high on interest, art and culture generally. Churches, galleries and architecture were important things to be seen. The route was carefully planned – and reading about the places they proposed to visit was very important in order that nothing should be missed. Each visit began by a night being spent with one of Margaret's friends who lived near where they were to catch the ferry. An early start meant that they needed to be as close as possible. I can remember hearing that on being asked when to expect them back, Margaret's reply on leaving home was: 'Expect us when you see us.' . . . And off they went.

Their trips usually lasted about three weeks – depending on where they went – and they often reduced us all to tears of laughter on their return when they told us about some of their adventures. On one of their earliest trips they were driving through the Simplon Pass in Switzerland – towing the caravan – when they looked out of the window and saw it overtaking them! It had jack-knifed, and caused a terrible traffic jam – with long-distance lorry drivers shaking their fists and shouting abuse. Eventually the problem was sorted out – and they continued on their journey. Little fazed them as they had brought up their families practically single-handedly during the Second World War and they were indomitable to say the least.

Another story I remember was how when the windscreen of the car broke during their return trip from Romania, they continued their drive with an umbrella up to keep off the rain! What an incredible sight this must have been.

On yet another occasion, I remember them telling us that they had got the caravan stuck on the steps of a church in St. Germain in Paris. Undaunted, Margaret went into the church and came out followed by a priest who crow-barred them off the steps and they continued on their way. There are many other stories which we all loved hearing and were unique in their originality and humour. What fun they had!

When my mother died in 1989, Margaret Guise came to her funeral, bringing a small posy of old fashioned roses that she had picked from her garden. By now she, too, was a very old lady.

She wrote me the most touching letter which I keep to this day in my Bible. In it, among many other kind and endearing things, she said: 'You can't live in a caravan without knowing people's failings but I don't believe your mother had any. She was always helpful and unselfish and such good company. It's not surprising she was so popular'.

When Margaret died shortly afterwards I went to her memorial service in Gloucester Cathedral. It was a marvellous celebration of her life and following it the family asked me to go back to Elmore for the wake. I wasn't sure that I could do this – as I had come down from London, where I was working – and wouldn't be able to catch a train back so easily without further transport. However, they assured me they could arrange this. So I went.

My mother Romie Stevens at her home in Frampton-on-Severn.

2.

Getting Married and Moving to Elmore

I had in my early twenties briefly gone out with John, Margaret's older son, who had lived at Elmore with his mother for a number of years since leaving the army. He had gone on to work for the Jockey Club as a starter and covered the entire country with meetings from Wincanton to Ayr – something that would be impossible to do these days with all the traffic.

We renewed our friendship – and were convinced our parents had fixed this from above! It was a very comfortable relationship – as we had known each other for a long time – albeit with a long break in the middle. I had also been partially brought up locally and so I had many friends in the area.

I was with John at Newbury on 18th July 1992 when he started his last race before retiring after twenty-five years. Both the *Racing Post* and the *Sporting Life* subsequently ran features on him, saying that his departure from racing was the end of an era. He had been extremely popular with both jockeys and trainers. Both newspapers mentioned some of the most eventful days of his career as a starter – some of which had been extremely funny. Indeed, as he pressed the lever to start the first race of his career the entire starting gate collapsed!

Sir John Guise starting his last race at Newbury in 1992.

Shortly after John's retirement from racing we got married, and I came to live at Elmore – which was a very happy and fulfilling period of my life. The community is a very small and close-knit one – and in completely rural England. Elmore, not far from Gloucester, is sandwiched between the River Severn and the Gloucester–Sharpness canal. The Guises have lived here for nearly 800 years and many of the families have also lived here for a very long time – which makes for a very solid community. I feel it is practically unique and we have a marvellous knack of all pulling together. There is a great deal of ability and talent in our community and we have a first-class choir in our church led by a very able choir mistress; also an excellent group of Village Players who put on a variety of productions during the year, and an exceptionally good and highly polished pantomime at Christmas. This, I especially love, with our farmers' sons playing the dames!

Our wedding was a very traditional country wedding and enormous fun. Two days beforehand we hosted a party in the house for the entire village community and their extended families. It was a very lively evening and towards the end of it John made a short speech where he thanked everyone for their support and very generous wedding present to us which was some Royal Worcester china. He finished with the reassuring words: 'And by the way, there won't be any changes!' Towards the back of the hall, a voice was heard to say: 'Changes! Changes! There haven't been any changes in Elmore for over 800 years!' What a wonderful thought.

Mr and Mrs William Stevens
request the pleasure of
your company at the marriage
of his sister
Sally
to
Sir John Guise Bt.
at St John the Baptist Church, Elmore
on Wednesday, 14th October 1992
at 2.30 o'clock
and afterwards at
Elmore Court

R.S.V.P
Elmore Court
Gloucester GL2 6NT

Top left: Elmore Church.

Top right: The vicar arrives.

Above: Elmore Church looking spendid.

Right: Sir John and his best man Dan Abbot.

Far right: The Ushers - left to right:
Brian Peace, David Stevens, John Penley, Jamie Guise, Richard Newell and Harry Dalzeal Payne.

Opposite page: Sally Stevens with her brother William arriving at the church.

The Reception at Elmore Court.

The happy couple leave for their honeymoon.

The Reception held in the Court.

At Christmas John and I took it in turns to have members of our respective families to stay. Elmore was a wonderful family home. I remember, in fact, staying there for Christmas before we got engaged and I lay in bed one morning counting up how many people were staying in the house. There were thirty-five! I can also remember waking up to the sound of children (John's great-nieces and great-nephews) running up and down the stairs shouting 'He's been!' meaning Father Christmas!

That year I gave John a Christmas stocking – not having seen him for a long time and not knowing what he would like. At the top I put a Father Christmas hat that I had bought from a barrow in Oxford Street just before I caught the train down from London on Christmas Eve. John wore it throughout the day on Christmas Day. He said he hadn't had a stocking for over forty years! And he was thrilled.

Being involved in racing, John naturally had many friends who were also involved in racing in various capacities. He stayed with some of his friends regularly as he travelled up and down the country starting races at the various meetings. He, in turn, held a large house-party for some of his closest friends for the National Hunt Meeting at Cheltenham – the Cheltenham Festival. Some of the guests had been staying at Elmore for this particular meeting for over thirty years and enjoyed looking back at the entries they had made in the Visitors Book. I can remember the first meeting that took place shortly after we were married when the house-party was considerably more at home at Elmore than I was – and it was a rather unnerving experience! However, once I got started with the restoration of the house, I began to feel more as if I belonged to it.

His Cheltenham house-parties were the highlight of John's year. He adored them and no detail was spared to make his friends feel welcome. We began getting the house ready ages in advance and everything was Spring-cleaned from top to bottom. As time went on I got better at co-hosting these house-parties as I began to get to know the ropes! They were always huge fun and much loved by our wonderful guests.

Elmore Court by Jim Cramsie

One weekend when we had guests staying, one of them asked if I had a deck chair – also a drawing pad and pencil. I had and I gave them to him. He then sketched this beautiful pencil drawing of the house. The friends were Jim and Rosie Cramsie. It was Jim who drew the picture and he is an untrained artist. Who could possibly have done better! I had his charming picture mounted and framed and also cards made from the image that I used for years when writing to friends and family.

Shortly after we were married, we were joined by a wonderful St.Helenian couple called Rex and Bronia Stevens. Bronia was our cook/housekeeper and Rex was our gardener/handyman. Bronia was only twenty-one when she and Rex arrived at Elmore, but they had already been married longer than we had! They were a wonderful addition to our lives and quite amazingly versatile.

Over the years they became very close to us – and ultimately our extended family. We had a wonderful relationship – each of us very respectful of the other and yet having a very relaxed relationship. Among his many talents Rex was very artistic. I can remember asking him on more than one occasion to do the flowers for me in the house. He did them beautifully. We used mainly foliage from the garden with a few flowers added – giving a very natural effect. At Christmas Rex and I would go to the aboretum at Westonbirt and buy Christmas trees for the house. Each Christmas we bought five trees and Rex seemed to take ages to choose the five he thought were best. When decorating them we used to get

so cold – as the house had so little heating – that I suggested we retire to the kitchen and warm by the AGA and have a cup of tea, I also suggested a splash of whisky in it to get our circulation going again. I used to say 'Rex, this isn't optional. It's compulsory!' He was highly amused and completely agreed. I can remember on another occasion saying to Bronia in a very light-hearted way 'Don't you think it is time we got Rex re-cycled!' 'Oh! I agree' said Bronia and we all laughed. In, fact we spent a huge amount of our time laughing – which was wonderful.

Rex and Bronia remained with us for about two-and-a-half years, following which they moved on to another family near London. They were succeeded by another St. Helenian couple called Derek and Delia Francis who again were a wonderful addition to our family. They in turn stayed with us, enhancing our lives in every way, until after about two years they decided to return to St. Helena to catch up with their families. In the fullness of time Rex and Bronia, who by now had a son, also returned to St. Helena to be reunited with their families, but when they heard that we were looking for help once more, they got in touch with us to ask if we would consider having them back with us. We were utterly delighted by this idea and wholeheartedly agreed for them to return. They then remained with us for the rest of my time at Elmore Court and we became even more fond of them – enjoying their help and watching their son grow into a most beautiful and highly intelligent little boy.

How lucky we were.

3.

The Restoration of Elmore

Returning from our honeymoon, we began the task of restoration and redecoration. Not much had been done for over a hundred years, so although the house had a wonderful atmosphere, it was more than a little in need of some attention!

When clearing out some of the cupboards, we made interesting discoveries. John's mother came from a generation that never threw anything away. I remember coming across a shoe box with the words: 'Pieces of string too short to be of any use' written by hand on the top with a fountain pen in John's mother's writing. Further investigation revealed several drawers with old housekeeping receipts.

Among the other interesting things we found were two charming boxes of lacemaking things – one with a musical box incorporated into it.

In further cupboards and drawers we found clothes belonging to various members of the family down the years and also those of some of the servants. I remember being particularly impressed by the magnificent materials used in the footmen's clothing; and again in the coachman's coat and breeches – all these were made by hand and had the most amazingly small stitches. The coachman's clothes were notably heavy materials, such as one would be unlikely to find these days when warm clothing is not so essential.

Another magnificent piece of work was the crewel-worked bedspread on the Oak Room bed. This depicted a tree which I suspect was either the Tree of Life or perhaps the Tree of Knowledge. I could be wrong. I always harboured a desire to take it to the Royal School of Needlework at Hampton Court to have it identified and restored, but unfortunately I never got as far as this. In such a big house with only a small team running it there was always more to do than there were hours in the day. I later had another bedspread made for daily use.

The first winter I spent at Elmore it was so cold in the house that I slept in two layers of long-sleeved, long-legged warm underwear with a scarf round my head. I can remember John saying: 'I am looking forward to the summer!' At the end of the winter I told John that I had decided I would spend the following winter with my sister and her husband who farmed in Devon. I said that I would return in the spring. Without saying a word, John arranged for some storage heaters to be fitted in our bedroom and also in the morning room – which made a huge difference. The house had a perfectly good – albeit antiquated – central heating system but it was fiendishly expensive to run, so we had only two radiators on in a house with about thirty-five rooms, unless we had an event in the house or guests staying – when the heating was put on for a short space of time.

One of the things we did a little later on, and which made a huge difference to the warmth of the house, was lining the ceiling of the cellar. The cellar was directly beneath the hall and the drawing room and open to the elements on three sides, so the drafts beforehand had been unbelievable. The cellar was actually one of the oldest parts of the house and was from the Tudor period.

However, in restoring the house the first thing to be addressed was updating the kitchen. It was an extraordinary sight with a completely antiquated system that was totally inadequate for the large gatherings that took place. Big family house parties at Christmas, large shooting parties throughout the season, regular charity events and John's much loved house parties for the Cheltenham Festival. It is inconceivable how meals for such events were prepared and produced. It was therefore enormously rewarding and fulfilling to be able to source and rebuild a workable kitchen and a very great relief to everyone involved that it was absolutely top priority.

John Lewis in Oxford Street London was the firm we chose. One of their kitchen designers had recently transformed the small kitchen in my London flat and it was he who we asked to turn his considerable skill and imagination to the kitchen at Elmore. It was an indisputable success and all the directors from the London store came down to inspect and admire it when it was finished. It was apparently the biggest kitchen they had ever done!

Their team that installed it and were magnificent in their speed and efficiency. As they were lodging at a pub in nearby Frampton and worked practically without a break throughout the day I made them their daily sandwiches and at the end of their week's work we invited them to ask their wives to come down from London to see what they had been doing. Having given them all lunch we then gave them a tour of the house. They loved it!

Second on the list for our attention, was the renovation of the dining room – almost as much in need of some tender loving care as the kitchen had been! I would say that this was probably the most rewarding of all the work we did – although it would have been a close-run thing with the kitchen.

In researching wallpapers, I chose Coles in London who are renowned for being the specialists for English country houses. Telephoning in advance of my visit I was given an appointment with their Mr Hills, a wonderful and extremely knowledgeable man in his seventies who was enormously kind and helpful.

Having taken with me pictures of the house and in particular the dining room, I brought home samples of possible wallpapers to show John, who after considerable thought chose the one we used. When I telephoned to order it I was told a batch of it was being printed at that moment. What a coincidence!

On one of my visits to Coles, I took with me a roll of the paper that had once covered the walls in the Oak Room – one of the main bedrooms of the house and which still had the original Tudor paintwork on the piece above the fireplace. I had found this huge roll of paper, which incidentally was backed with canvas, in the attic. I asked Mr. Hills if this paper may have originally come from Coles. He looked at it thoughtfully and said . 'No. It is French and hand painted'. That, too, was very interesting.

Elmore Court Dining Room prior to re-decoration, on the walls are many family portraits including one of Sir John as a boy (above right).

Opposite page: Work begins with the redecoration of the dining room. Rex Stevens repaints the curtain hooks. Bronia Stevens oversees Mr Duffield and his nephews rehanging the paintings.

Above: The dining room reinstated.

Right: John and Zamara in the hall.

Further projects John and I turned our attention to were new chair covers in the Drawing Room – a fabric that was especially printed for the room. New curtains and bedspreads in the bedrooms and further new wallpapers too. Some of the previous wallpapers were very old and interesting. In fact, everything to do with the restoration of the house was fascinating and a great privilege to be involved in. Over the following years the house began to look much more loved. I did the recce and John, in the main, made the final selection. It all came together very satisfactorily and seemed much appreciated and admired by our families, friends and the village community. Although as John once said: 'We like it and that's all that matters!'

THE GATES

The magnificent wrought iron gates designed by Jean Tijou and made in Bristol for the Guise family in 1716 by William Edney of Bristol, are a copy of the imposing gate screens leading to the Park at Hampton Court.

They originally stood at Rendcombe Park a large property in the Cotswolds owned by the Guise family. However, when Rendcombe was sold in the 19th century the gates were brought to Elmore, which was to become the family's chief residence. There were no motorised vehicles in those days so the gates – having been dismantled – would have been brought to Elmore on a series of horse-drawn vehicles which would have been an extraordinary sight even at that time.

When John and I married, the gates (like much of the rest of the house) were greatly in need of restoration and in 1998, with the help of English Heritage, work began to restore them to their former glory. This proved to be no small task. Keith Blakeney, a wrought iron specialist, who had previously worked for English Heritage and recently set up his own foundry in Buckinghamshire, was chosen by English Heritage to undertake the work. He immersed himself body and soul in the work, which he found both hugely interesting and greatly fulfilling. He spent the following three-and-a-half years deeply committed to the task.

During this time John and I – sometimes together with John's sister Philippa Fraser and also Harry Dalzell Payne – a long time army friend of John's who had a flat in the house – visited the foundry on many occasions to see the progress of the work. It was a privilege to watch and listen to Keith's findings. Part of his discovery was that, interestingly, over a period of several hundred years, the gates had been painted no fewer than eight different colours. This was a discovery Keith made when stripping them down. They had at one time been emerald green, another buttercup yellow yet another time they had been white – always heavily gilded at the top. What an extraordinary sight they would have been in some of these colours – and so conspicuous. However, they would have stood at the entrance to a pretty imposing property which Rendcombe Park most certainly would have been at that time.

Before the gates were removed, I wrote to every household in the village telling them that the gates were going to be taken down and sent away for restoration. Their dismantling would be a once in a lifetime spectacle and interesting to watch. Subsequently we held a picnic at the gates for the spectators!

Keith Blakeney was hugely interested in the work that he was entrusted with. He became deeply immersed mentally, emotionally and physically in the fascination of the work he was carrying out. He involved us in all his findings, thoughts and work. It was an enormous privilege.

One of the things that particularly interested Keith when working on the gates was the fact that the swan on top of the gates – part of the family crest – was hollow inside and that it contained a time capsule recording the work that had been done previously to the gates; this he read with great interest, carefully putting it back in place afterwards. He then added another, describing the work that he had carried out. How fascinating this is.

Following their restoration during 1998 to 2002 and their return to Elmore, it took a considerable time for them to be set up, and part of the final painting was done on site. John chose the colour for the final coats of paint – a subtle shade of dark grey-green – and was well pleased with the result when the work was completed. But as with everything, restoration becomes upkeep and this is ongoing.

Above: Undergoing restoration at the workshops.

Left & opposite: Gates being disassembled in preparation for restoration.

The gates restored to their former glory.

4.
Country Pursuits

The Guise family has enjoyed a traditional sporting life for a very long time. Indeed, records show that there was a regular shoot on the estate as far back as the mid eighteen hundreds. Today, there is still an Elmore shoot; however, it is a much higher profile event – and at the end of the season there is always a meet of the Berkeley Foxhounds – and so it was the first spring I was at Elmore following our marriage.

We not only hosted meets of the Berkeley Foxhounds but also the Leadon Vale Bassett Hounds. All these were well attended and much enjoyed events in our sporting year and particularly enjoyed by our local community.

For a while deerhound coursing was also part of our sporting calendar.

SHOOTING

Shooting has been an integral part of the Guise family's sporting life for many years, with records showing that there was a regular shoot on the estate as early as 1884.

Before the Second World War, Sir Anselm Guise – my father in law – ran a shoot consisting of five guns in total. These were a small group of his friends and they shot for the pot. The bag included wild fowl, duck and snipe – which are migratory.

Sometime after the Second World War, Michael Watts, one of the estate farm tenants, became involved in the shoot which at that time was a farmers' shoot.

John's younger brother Jamie, who had been working in Rhodesia and South Africa for a number of years, returned to England and in the mid-eighties became involved in the Elmore shoot. It was then that Jamie and Michael Watts joined forces and considerably upgraded the shoot. It was a driven shoot with reared birds – Jamie and Michael each shooting equal numbers of days with a total of a mere sixteen days per season. Michael Watts ran the shoot – something he has done very ably over the years.

In the late eighties a number of extensive further improvements were made and since then the shoot has been steadily improving in every way. Since I came to Elmore the shoot has had three keepers – all of whom have been highly competent and extremely nice. Currently the shoot has a first-class keeper – Kevin Jarrod – who is also in charge of a great team of beaters and pickers-up. It is a very highly respected shoot and great fun.

Kevin Jarrod - the current keeper.

Currently Jamie provides guns on eight days and Michael the remaining days. There are approximately thirty days shooting per season – including Beater's Day which, in my view, is one of the highlights of the season with lots of light-hearted banter and some seriously competent shooting.

Throughout our married life John and I welcomed Jamie's shooting parties to the house during the season, where they lunched and later had tea before choosing their birds and going home. They were days we hugely enjoyed and most of Jamie's guests were regulars and became great friends of ours, too.

On a shooting morning John regularly got up at 6.00 a.m. (something he didn't otherwise do!) and came downstairs to light the drawing room fire to warm the otherwise extremely cold room. He then oversaw the progress of the fire until further help was on duty. He never failed in this job – or in many others. He was meticulously punctual and reliable in all things.

My husband John had been a keen shot and a very good one, but after breaking his back hunting in Ireland and again at a race meeting in England where he was the starter, he found he could no longer swing a gun. So he gave his matching pair of Purdey guns to his brother, Jamie.

Kevin Jarrod, Paul Browning, Bob Smith and Frank Sneddon.

Simon Smith at the end of a day's beating.

The beaters.

Rev Thomas Woodhouse enjoys some refreshment.

Top and above: Jamie Guise.

Above: The guns assemble.

Left: Carole Guise with her dogs.

Below: Michael Watts.

Keeper Kevin Jarrod prepares for the 2009 season.

Top right: Pheasants at 6 weeks in their rearing pen.

Right: Week old ducks in the safety of the shed.

Below & right: Releasing partridges into the game crop.

THE BERKELEY FOXHOUNDS

The Elmore estate lies to the northern end of the Berkeley Hunt country and has for hundreds of years been host to some excellent days' foxhunting.

The Berkeley Hounds – one of the oldest packs of foxhounds in the country – are owned by the Berkeley family and are kennelled a short distance across the lower meadows from Berkeley Castle, a mere fifteen miles from Elmore. The masters and hunt servants wear the family livery of musk. The 5th Earl of Berkeley (1745-1810) hunted his hounds from Berkeley in Gloucestershire to Berkeley Square in London and then hunted them back again – usually taking about six weeks.

Shortly after we were married, a meet card arrived with the morning post and John announced at breakfast that the Berkeley Hounds were meeting at Elmore the following Wednesday.

'Oh! Good', I said. 'How lovely. What shall we give them?'

'They don't come through the Gates' John said. 'They never have'.

'We'll have to change all that!' I said. And from then on, for many years, we had great pleasure in entertaining them. Something that also gave pleasure to the entire local community.

On more than one occasion we disturbed the garden fox and I remember clearly Chris Maiden, who was huntsman at the time, getting a fox to jump off the ivy-covered wall at the back of the walled garden – much to the amusement of John Berkeley.

On another occasion the Berkeley Hunt had invited the Taunton Vale Foxhounds to have a day's hunting in this country. A huge gathering took place at Elmore that day. Not only had the mounted members of their hunt travelled up from Devon and Somerset for the day, but a considerable number of their foot followers also came – much to the pleasure of their joint master, Robin Kemp. Following the meet, one hundred and seventeen horses went out through the gates to follow hounds and enjoy their day! I got added pleasure from Robin Kemp's visit – as I remembered him from childhood days many years before.

Elmore, lying on the edge of the River Severn, has many of its fields divided by rhynes – small tributaries – which have historically provided wonderful jumps for the field and on occasions continue to do so. However, whereas once they were dug out by hand, making for more gradual slopes at the edge, they are now dug out by machines and are far less friendly to jump.

There have always been garden foxes at Elmore and I can remember on one occasion looking through my bedroom window and, because the garden was floodlit at night by security lights, being able to witness the courtship of a garden vixen who subsequently gave birth to four cubs who she proudly entertained on the lawn in front of the house . . . in broad daylight!

There is a magic about Elmore – in so many ways. I have also seen skirmishes between young dog foxes competing for a vixen in the early hours of a morning – completely oblivious of being watched.

There are many stories I could tell about the lives and activities of foxes in the garden at Elmore – all of them wonderful.

Sir John and Mrs John (Gina) Berkeley.

Gina Berkeley, Sir John Guise and Jenny Watts.

Above: David Skinner and Brian Savage.

Above: Lt. Colonel Roger Ker, Alli Long and Ros Jones.

Below: Rollo Clifford MFH and Sarah Clifford arriving at the meet at Elmore Court.

Past hunt secretary Ian Shaw.

Michael (Mike) Good.

Below: Huntsman Chris Maiden (left) with whipper in Ben Slee (right). In the foreground Tom Chamberlayne with his grand daughter Rachel.

Jamie Guise with Francis Penley.

Sally offers refreshment to John Penley.

Above: Chris Maiden and Ben Slee about to move off.
Below: John Berkeley with his hounds and huntsman.

Below: Sir John Guise, Rollo Clifford and John Berkeley.

Above: Sir John Guise and John Berkeley.　　　　　　　　　　*Below: Major-General Harry Dalzell-Payne chats with Jamie Guise.*

DEERHOUND COURSING MEETINGS

Following the arrival of our first deerhound, Chapel Tower Zamara, we welcomed the Deerhound Club Coursing Members. Their first meeting at Elmore was in 1996 and apart from my bitch being in season at the time and being unable to take part we had a thoroughly enjoyable time.

We had as many people as we could fit in the house to stay the night before – which was great fun and on the day hares abounded. In one field alone no fewer than five hares showed themselves. There followed some interesting coursing for the two that were slipped – as they got so excited that they had some very original ideas about the plan! We broke for lunch and had a picnic in the field, and at the end of the day everyone came back to the house for high tea and enthused about the day. There was just as much noise as there would have been at one my children's parties.

Deerhounds course their quarry and are slipped two at a time, one wearing a white collar and the other a red. The judge, who on this occasion was mounted on a horse kindly loaned by David Guilding, rode at the top of the respective field and the hounds were judged on performance. We had, I think, only two days like this before the hunting ban and were then forced to do a farm walk instead where we walked our hounds on leads across our land and along the river bank. On one occasion we followed the walk with a visit to Berkeley Castle's deer park where needless to say we did not take our hounds!

Note.
Deerhounds are one of the oldest breeds of hunting hounds. They are sight hounds and historically were called such names as Rough Coated Greyhounds and Highland Greyhounds. Not until much later were they called Deerhounds. Although their origins are lost in the mists of time there are chronicles of the existence of similar types of hounds as early as 300 A.D. They were used in the Highlands of Scotland for hunting red deer. They were worked as a brace with one being slipped to single out the quarry and later the second, and together they brought the animal down and went for a quick kill – usually taking the quarry by the throat. Working them was a highly skilled job and very dangerous. The hounds had to be extremely courageous. They had to have speed, endurance, strength – and great courage.

With the introduction of firearms Deerhounds lost their purpose and were largely replaced by other types of dogs who were used to track injured deer.

Historically no one, unless they were a nobleman, was allowed to own a Deerhound and many Kings and Queens of England have much enjoyed their sport.

In the 1950s, Kenneth Cassels – a key member of the Deerhound Club – introduced hare coursing – which was highly popular until the hunting ban in 2005.

Mr Bernard Hendy, one of the stewards.

BY INVITATION: a DEERHOUND COURSING MEETING under Deerhound Club and NCC Rules

Saturday 30th November 1996
at Elmore, Gloucester
By kind permission of Sir John & Lady Guise

Judge: Mrs. Jenny Loch

Slipper: Mr. Guy Tompkins

STEWARDS: Dr. Helps, Mr. Cassels, Mrs. Dowsett, Miss Girling, Mr. Hendy
CARD STEWARD: Ms. Brooks.

Picker Up: Mr. Chastney.

After a brief instruction class . . .

. . . they set off. Centre of photo: Mr Kenneth Cassels.

Above: Keeping a good line at a 'walked up coursing meeting.   Below: Enthusiastic owners walking ahead of the line, hoping to spot a hare.

Above - Awaiting loose hounds to be collected up after a course.

LEADON VALE BASSET HOUNDS

Beginning in the late 1990s/early 2000s we also welcomed the Leadon Vale Basset Hounds. What charming individuals they are, so appealing to all ages and a wonderful height for children to enjoy at the meet.

Originally a privately owned pack and founded in 1967 by David Mann using French Artesian Normand bassets they are now run by a committee – but the aim remains still to breed the French style of basset.

They were traditionally used to hunt hares and are well built to be able to cover heavy plough and get through hedges and over fences. They work in a similar way to beagles. However the advantage of bassets is that they hunt more slowly and methodically which enables you to see more hound work and watch the skill of their hunting. There are now only seven registered packs of basset hounds in the UK.

We gave lawn meets at the house for a number of years until my husband died. We enjoyed having them enormously and would go out and watch them work in the meadows below. I remember one year when the master and whippers-in – together with a small group of followers – came to thank us at the end of their day. We invited them in for a spur of the moment high tea of boiled eggs and fruit cake. What fun that was for all of us . . . and a day we still remember.

The crowd gathers at Elmore Court.

Steven Evans, Huntsman, Lady Sally, Gee Kimblewick, Whipper in.

Leadon Vale Eric meets some supporters.

Hunt staff, hounds and supporters of the Leadon Vale at the Elmore Court Lawn Meet.

Steven Evans, Huntsman keeping a watchful eye on the hounds.

Above: Leadon Vale Eric meets another young supporter. Below: Gee Kimblewick Michael Whitehead Steven Evans and followers moving off.

5.
Village Life . . . with all its activities

Shortly after we were married, Barbara Taylor, the head teacher of the local primary school in the neighbouring village of Longney invited me to open their annual fete. This, I was delighted to do and during the afternoon judged the fancy dress competition – always full of fun and imagination.

Returning home, I thought our own garden would be the perfect place to hold a village fete and I asked John if we could do so. In complete agreement, he began to draw up a list of people from our village community and form a committee. Plans began to be laid for the following summer.

Our village fete was a great success and enjoyed by many people not only in our community – but far beyond. We followed this up with a hog roast and a dance in the house for those who had helped with the day. It was wonderful fun – and utterly exhausting! We decided that with such a small village community we should not hold another for at least five years. This proved to be a good idea.

Preparations for the 1995 Elmore Village Fete.

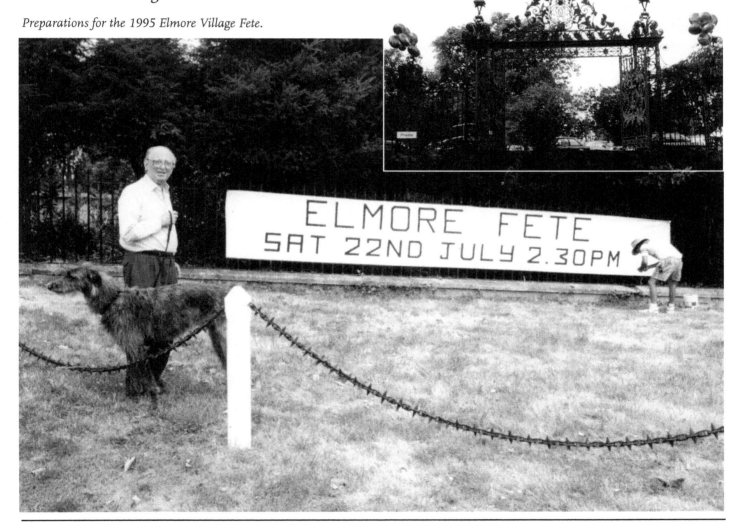

Above: The Team - Brenda Lovell, Marjorie Longney and Mona Robertson. Below: Pony rides. Opposite page: The Raffle being drawn.

RAFFLE PRIZES

1ST.	SIX MAGNUMS OF CLARET.
2ND	SALMON CAUGHT ON THE RIVER SPEY IN SCOTLAND
3RD	TWO TICKETS FOR THE MEMBERS ENCLOSURE AT NEWBURY RACES. ON A DAY OF YOUR CHOICE
4TH	MAGNUM OF CHAMPAGNE
5TH	KING SIZE DUVET.
6TH	LITRE OF WHISKEY.

Dancers at the Elmore Fete.

May 1995 - 50th Anniversary of V.E. Day on top of Windmill Hill) (also known as Scar Hill).

Falklands victory celebrations - Elmore was one of the official beacons.

Father Christmas at the Children's Party.

Later that year I decided to give a children's Christmas party for all the children in Elmore. I added to these the children of the local chimney sweep; he had recently swept the chimney for Father Christmas to come down; and the daughter of the man who did our contract gardening. It was huge fun – and no one enjoyed it more than I did! Fifty-seven children between the ages of three weeks and seventeen years came to the party. I divided them into age groups and asked various members of our village community to organize them in different rooms in the house. I gave them a list of suggestions for games to play together with a tray of prizes. I gave similar parties every second year and the years between we entertained the entire village community to a Christmas lunch. These were wonderful gatherings and everyone pulled together and enjoyed themselves every bit as much as we enjoyed having them.

Playing games at the Christmas party.

At that time there was a competition for the Best Kept Village in Gloucestershire with a trophy and sign placed on the village green of the winning village. For several years we were lucky enough to win this and proudly enjoyed the recognition by displaying the sign.

In the summer of 1995 Elmore was one of the official beacons for the country's celebration of the fiftieth anniversary of V.E. Day. As light faded we lit our bonfire on Windmill Hill, sang songs and had a picnic by the light of the fire. Again great fun was had and another milestone marked

Summer 1998 was the start of an important and enormously enjoyable period in the lives of our community. We were told that we were going to have a new vicar and, after the official procedure of selection headed by the then Archdeacon of Gloucester, the Venerable Christopher Wagstaff, and

Elmore winner of the Bledisloe Cup competition 2001 for the small villages section. CPRE Member Judge Gabriel Hutton speaking to the assembled villagers prior to the presentation of the Winner's Cup and Plaque to Graham Littleton (seated) Chair of Elmore Parish Council.

Below: Sir John Guise with Graham Littleton, Chair of Elmore Parish Council.

Residents of Elmore winner of the Bledisloe Plate for the Best Kept Village in Gloucestershire in 1995.

my husband John – who at the time was patron of the living, and assisted by the current churchwardens of the day, Thomas Woodhouse was duly selected. He took up his post that autumn and for the following very special seven years we enjoyed the guidance of Thomas in our daily lives. He brought with him his young wife Kate and their baby daughter Charlotte – a family that grew in size considerably while they were with us. How we loved them!

Dispite not having come from a rural background, Thomas embraced the life completely and was soon to be seen out at our lawn meets for the Berkeley Foxhounds and also out with the guns on Beaters' Day. This was a day towards the end of the shooting season when those who have helped to provide sport for the regular shooting parties are given a day when it is their turn to enjoy the sport. They are treated royally with all the same privileges given to the regular guns – those who shoot throughout the rest of the season. Thomas immersed himself in rural life – and we adored him for it.

On Christmas Day – a busy day in the life of a vicar – Thomas and his entire family joined us each year for Christmas lunch at Elmore Court and, having previously been a chef, he was fully up to carving one of the two turkeys we had for Christmas lunch. The Woodhouses became firmly part of our family – and to this day remain very close friends.

The Millennium was another opportunity for our village community to pull together. We had a marquee on the lawn and a huge celebration. In the hall of the house and down the drive we had a wonderful exhibition of memorabilia from many of the houses and farms in the village. A number of them have been in the same families for hundreds of years, an extraordinary situation that is almost unique these days. After the Millennium celebrations I felt perhaps the children could have enjoyed something specifically for them, so I held a sports day for them in the garden with old-fashioned races such as three-legged races, egg and spoon races and of course running races. This was again a huge success and again great fun.

When I first read about locally-based Gifford's circus in our county magazine I felt compelled to go. I couldn't imagine enjoying it on my own, so I gathered all the children who were at home on that particular weekend and who usually came to my children's Christmas parties, and I took them with me. How we enjoyed it! I have not missed one of their tours since.

On one occasion a group of children from a neighbouring urban community who were being shown life in a rural village visited Elmore for the day. I took them round the house and introduced them to my deerhounds – which took their real interest! They so enjoyed their visit one of them endearingly told me she would like to come and live here with us. I said to her, 'that's a lovely idea but don't you think Mummy would miss you?' 'No' the child said, 'she wouldn't'. How very sad I thought. The children all wrote afterwards to thank me for their visit and every one of the thank yous had wonderful illustrations – chiefly of the deerhounds! The visit of these children was only one of the many incidents that enriched our lives on a daily basis.

Elmore Millennium celebrations.

Another I remember with amusement was when I heard a knock on the side door one afternoon and opened it to Lawrence Bennett, a very small boy who lived opposite the gates of the Court. 'Hello Lawrence,' I said. 'How lovely to see you. What can I do for you?' 'We've run out of eggs' he said. 'Could you let me have some please?' 'Certainly' I said. 'come in. How many would you like?'. I put some in a basket and off he went. How wonderful I thought. He didn't go to the house next door – instead he walked up the drive and came to us. That boy will go far I thought! Later when we were holding various fund raising events at the house I, in turn, turned to the boys in the village – as they grew up – and asked them to help with parking the cars. We all helped each other. There was a great spirit.

John Camm, one of our tenant farmers and a much loved member of our community, provided us all with lamb for our deep freezes throughout the year. Also turkeys at Christmas – and eggs and potatoes for those who wanted them.

John Camm.

Rodney Williams soaks matting with disinfectant on the road into the village during the foot and mouth outbreak of 2001.

Crisis came when, in February 2001, foot and mouth disease hit the UK. Within two weeks seventy farms in the UK had been hit and their entire livestock destroyed. What a terribly bitter blow it was and such tragic stories unfolded by the day. In order to protect our estate farms, John held a meeting of our tenant farmers and set out a plan of action for our village. It was decided that we should have notices made preventing anyone except residents from coming through the village and carpets soaked in disinfectant nailed to the road through which all vehicles travelled. Miraculously, Elmore escaped the horrors of what so many others succumbed to. How lucky we were.

Further village activities included scarecrow competitions and flower festivals, all of them great opportunities for gatherings together and tremendous fun.

On one occasion when I was making a scarecrow of our gamekeeper, Kevin, I asked Bob – who is a great friend and who mows the lawn for me amongst many other things – whether he had his tool box with him to which he replied he had. 'Why?' He asked. I said I was having difficulty in keeping Kevin's trousers up and I wanted him to put a screw through the back of Kevin's trousers and attach them to the main body of the scarecrow. Bob deftly replied: 'All keepers have difficulty in keeping their trousers up!' This was typical of Bob's ready wit and mischievous sense of humour.

John and I hosted a number of events for local charities all of which we enjoyed – particularly spectacular was Beating the Retreat, which was performed on the lawn in front of the house and carried out by the Royal Gloucestershire Hussars who have their museum in Gloucester Docks. This regiment was later amalgamated with the Wiltshire Yeomanry to become The Royal Wessex Yeomanry.

A very moving service was held in Gloucester Cathedral when the announcements of the amalgamations were made and many elderly men broke down in tears at the apparent loss of their beloved regiments.

We hosted a garden festival in aid of the British Heart Foundation. This brought a local silver band which sounded very appealing. In addition, we hosted a large number of fundraising events in the house – which were all very popular.

From time to time we took parties of people round the house, many of them with considerable historical knowledge. How interesting for us that was.

Scarecrow of the Game Keeper - with his trousers up!

Who am I? - Lady Guise.

Scarecrow of John Camm.

6.

The Garden . . . and Jerusalem

The first signs of the garden waking up after the winter are the snowdrops appearing, covering large areas under the trees – a very welcome sight. This is followed by a magical display of aconites spread generously beneath the copper beech tree to the left of the front of the house. Then the daffodils appear and are a breath-taking sight in the long grass beyond the lawn as you look from the house down towards the main gates and way out to the right. During our married life John and I added to these by many hundreds.

In May cow parsley appears in the long grass with bluebells and cowslips, which together make a very romantic picture. At the same time the double flowering cherry trees blossom, adding to the romance.

The magnolia trees – of which there are many – and the lilac all begin to come out; also the wisteria. I think May is a wonderful time of the year. So much is happening . . . and there is so much still to come.

The nine acres of garden are of an informal layout with a large lawn in front of the house extending to the longer grass beyond.

Many years ago the garden was mainly grass and trees. There were two tennis courts laid out in front of the house. Later, when flowers became fashionable, the border was added down one side of the drive and flowers and shrubs were planted. There is a walled garden to one side of

the house which originally contained a number of greenhouses. John told me that some of them had grown peaches and nectarines. By the time I was married these had all disappeared and, although the walled garden had once grown vegetables, it was no longer possible to keep this going with our limited help and eventually we decided to grass it over.

I subsequently planted a small area of fruit trees which were all old-fashioned varieties: greengages, damsons, apples (including Elmore Pippin) and pears, which included an ancient variety called Black Worcester. These were edged with quince and medlar, both of which have the most wonderful blossom.

SIGNIFICANT TREES

Approaching the house from the main gates there is a tulip tree on the right hand side of the drive. Further back on the same stretch is an ancient mulberry tree; onwards from here is a catalpa tree and not far from this a magnificent cedar. At one time this had a small plaque on the ground in front of it stating that it had been planted to commemorate the twenty-first birthday of the son of General Sir John Guise.

The copper beech, already mentioned, is of very beautiful proportions and hugely complementary to the house. Further round the side of the house near the stables is a plane tree with its wonderful gnarled bark.

Probably one of the most significant of all is the horse chestnut tree in front of and at the corner of the pond garden. John told me – and his father had told him – that this is the tree beneath which Hubert Parry was sitting when he composed the music for 'Jerusalem'. Naturally, we included this hymn in our wedding service.

Further on round the garden in the area of longer grass there are three other large trees in a group: a horse chestnut, a copper beech and an oak tree. These, my sister-in-law Philippa Fraser told me, had been planted by her and her two brothers – my husband John and brother Jamie – when they were children and, because their parents had been sure the trees wouldn't grow particularly well, they had been planted more or less out of sight of the house. However, they all did extremely well and grew into very fine trees indeed – albeit possibly a little too close together!

The pond garden is a charming area, with a sycamore tree growing rather haphazardly and leaning across it. The pond slopes gradually into the water from either end with cobbled stones leading into a shallow, flat-bottomed narrow stretch of water. It was, I believe, originally built to wash the carriages which would have been driven slowly through it in the process.

Years before we were married there had

apparently been a little summer house at the far end, but there is nothing left of it any longer, and a silver birch tree grows there instead. However, it was a lovely idea.

Shortly after we married we added another border between the copper beech tree and the entrance to the pond garden. Here I planted delphiniums, lupins, and hollyhocks, many of which I grew from seed. One of our wedding presents was a fig tree, and this we planted at the back of the border and added a clematis. There is nearly always something of interest in bloom in the garden.

Against the side of the house – on the left hand wall as you face the house –there is a blue wisteria. This was falling forwards when I was first married, but we attached it to the wall again and it flowered in abundance thereafter. There is a white wisteria growing up a high wall in the walled garden, where the greenhouse had previously stood growing nectarines and

peaches, another magnificent sight when it is in bloom. Both of these have very pretty leaves after the flowers have disappeared and I used them frequently with a variety of other leaves for foliage in house arrangements, and also when I was doing the church flowers. There is a second fig tree in the walled garden together with two magnolia trees.

John's mother had been a keen and very knowledgeable gardener and had worked on her hands and knees tirelessly tending her beloved garden almost to the end of her life. She had been particularly fond of her old-fashioned roses and I remember she brought a small bunch of them with her when she came to my mother's funeral. However, after she died the garden became very neglected, and when John realized something had to be done he employed outside help to clear the wilderness that the border had largely become, and to replant it. Sadly the old fashioned roses were removed.

After we were married, John and I went to David

Austen one day in early summer when the roses there were at their best, and we began a new collection of roses that we added to year by year. Many of them thereafter came from Mr. Marshall's nursery at North Nibley – where it was such a pleasure to talk to him. He was so knowledgeable and so kind. The first time I visited him I took photographs of the garden at Elmore to illustrate where I wanted to put roses. I told him that I knew little about gardening but that I was very interested. He told me that it didn't matter at all not being knowledgeable. All

that mattered was that I was interested! We formed an excellent friendship.

Later on I visited Mottisfont Abbey near Romsey in Hampshire where the national collection of old roses is kept. I went with a friend, Cecelia Campbell, and we had a wonderful time. We arrived in the early evening, as had been suggested to me, and had a picnic in the car park before going round the garden. We had the garden practically to ourselves.

Having seen here what a great effect roses have when grown up walls, I bought three Constance Spry roses and planted them side by side on the far side of the walled garden from the house. I planted further rambling roses (Rambling Rector, Bobby James, and Seagull, which are all very similar in appearance) around the other walls of the walled garden. Eventually they have grown into the most wonderful display. I planted another climbing rose, Himalayan Musk, up the sycamore tree that leant over the pond garden. It grew so well it looked as if the tree was in blossom when the rose was in flower.

I loved planting roses on walls, and sometimes I underplanted them with clematis. I did this very successfully, I thought, with Gloire de Dijon rose and Ville de Lyon clematis, amongst others.

Other charming aspects of the garden are the pair of small copses on either side of the main gates, one having an abundance of aconites in the Spring; also the gravestones of many of the beloved animals belonging to the family who had died over the years.

I always felt that one of the most endearing things was that the family had never considered that either the house or the garden were too precious for people to enjoy themselves. This added enormously to their appeal and meant that everyone could feel relaxed.

Above: Roses growing along the walls of the Walled Garden.   *Below: Fruit trees newly planted in the Walled Garden.*

Lupins and delphiniums in all their splendour.

Dephiniums, lupins and hollyhocks flourishing in the border between copper beech tree and pond garden.

7.
The Deerhounds

Elmore is not only a wonderful family home; at one time I believe that it had been a hunting lodge.

I had for some time been thinking about having a dog. It was such a perfect place to have one, and we had always had dogs at home when I was growing up. It was a question now of what sort of dog would be most suitable for us. We had a very large garden and wonderful places to walk. One of the guns, Derek Goode, a great friend who shot regularly at Elmore and whose young labrador bitch I had admired, offered to give me one of her puppies when she whelped. Our gamekeeper at the time had also suggested to me that if I were to have a gun dog he would teach it to 'pick up'. Although going out with the guns on a shooting day was one of the things I enjoyed, I felt however that everyone around seemed to have a gun dog and I rather wanted to be different.

After our marriage we were regularly invited to lunch with a wonderful old lady called Joan Dunn, who had lived locally all her married life. She had, been married twice. Her first husband was Claude de Lisle Bush, and at that time she lived at Eastington Park; following his death she married Brigadier Keith Dunn. She had been a keen hunting woman all her life and had hunted with the Berkeley Foxhounds. She had a passion for the Berkeley Marsh. She had also had her own pack of Basset hounds. When Joan and her husband gave up foxhunting Joan took to deerhounds, and with her husband Keith coursed them for many years at Dava in Scotland where they enjoyed the friendship of Anastasia Noble of Ardkinglas. Miss Noble was from one of the old Scottish families who had done much to save the breed from extinction during and following the Second World War, when they ceased to be used to hunt deer.

John and I were invited to lunch with Joan once a fortnight. By this time she was wheelchair-bound and found it easier for friends to visit her than for her to visit them. It was while talking to her and listening to her experiences that I began to think that deerhounds would be perfect at Elmore. We had such a wonderful set up for them. I also felt that I had married into one of the oldest families in England, the Guises (de Gyse as they were originally), who had come over with William the Conqueror. For this reason, and because we lived in a house steeped in history, it seemed appropriate to have a dog with history. Deerhounds are one of the oldest breeds of hunting hounds.

Joan was delighted at my interest in deerhounds and was quick to get in touch with her old friend Anastasia Noble (known to her close friends as Tasia), since she had bred deerhounds for many years. I arranged to meet her at the Game Fair, which that year was being held at Cornbury Park in Oxfordshire, and was on our way home from staying with friends for Goodwood Races. We duly met up and during our conversation I asked her if there would be a chance of her letting me have a bitch puppy. She told me that she had a bitch in whelp at the time and would have a word in her ear! 'It would,' she said, 'be the twenty-sixth request for a bitch puppy!' I remember John saying to her: 'How shall we know when the bitch has given birth? Will there be a notice the *The Times*?' 'Good Heavens, no!' said Miss Noble. 'The *Scottish Daily Record*, more likely!'

In the event the bitch failed to give birth and Miss Noble recommended me to someone called Jenefer Cooper who lived in Herefordshire; she, Miss Noble told me, had a bitch whom she knew was in whelp. And so it was that I met Jenefer – and her deerhound bitch Ardkinglas Polka with her litter of eight puppies. With amazing generosity, Jenefer offered me the pick of the litter – a bitch puppy called Zamara. Chapeltower Zamara came to us at four months and was the start of my deerhounds at Elmore. She fitted into our lives perfectly and seemed destined to live in such a beautiful house. She taught me how to look after her, which on reflection is really quite funny. I might add I had a lot of really good advice from friends, including Miss Noble, but Zamara's tuition was immediate and on site! She had a great sense of humour, but also of presence. She considered herself above discipline and went on to become a Grand Duchess quite naturally!

In her prime I think Zamara was the most beautiful creature I ever saw. However, showing was not for her. The first time I took her to a show was the Deerhound Club Breed Show at Llandrindod Wells in 1995 where Dr. Poyner-Wall was judging. As it was the first time I had ever been to a hound show I did not know what was expected and naturally did not do justice to Zamara. Neither was she very

co-operative! But I remember that, seeing I was in a certain amount of difficulty and after placing her second in the Puppy Bitch Class, Dr.Poyner-Wall suggested that I persevere with her as she told me she was 'very nice'. I took Zamara to a few more shows but she hated it. On seeing me putting the show bag ready in preparation to go to a show she decided to hide – as much as to say 'You can go if you like but I shall stay behind!' In the end I decided there was no point in taking her as she disliked it so much, so after that I went without her. I attended a few more shows on my own so that I could learn a bit more about the breed.

Zamara loved her home and our land with the quarries of foxes and hares. She undoubtedly had a wonderful life – but she was lonely. She had always longed for puppies and I had taken her to a number of stud dogs but so far without success. She loved it when Jenefer called in for a while to Elmore on their way home from a show and brought Zog, Zamara's litter brother. Andrew Chastney, a friend who lived a few miles away, also used to call in from time to

- 70 -

Left - Zamara 'at home' at Elmore Court.   Above - in full flight!

time with his two deerhounds and a lurcher, and we'd take them all for a walk. Zamara used to get so excited at their visits she would race across the lawn to the main gates to greet them.

Lushinghay Fiducia came into our lives at the age of three. She was a rescue dog and was already on her second home. We became her third. She was related to Zamara whose litter sister was her mother. Caroline Dowsett's dog Terreclien Osrich was her sire and it was Caroline who contacted me and told me of her plight. She was being advertised in a local newspaper as being for sale and Caroline appealed to me to go and see her. Somerset, which was where Fiducia was, no more than an hour and a half's drive away so I agreed and set off with our gardener at the time, a particularly good chap called Paul. We duly arrived at the house, having previously telephoned to make an appointment.

Fiducia was brought out for us to see and was deeply touching in her appeal for help. Poor thing she could hardly stand and smelled unbelievably awful. She had had her tail slammed in a door and it remained misshapen for the rest of her life. She was

so pathetic. I went home and thought it through and returned the following day to collect her and bring her to Elmore. I had to bath her twice before even taking her to the vet as she smelled so awful. The vet found she had fleas so large that he thought they were ticks. She also had a skin irritation and scratched constantly. I took her to the very highly respected homeopathic vet Richard Allport, and with his great knowledge and skill he managed to cure her completely of her skin irritation, although this took some time.

Zamara was undoubtedly a prima donna. She was also lonely and this was perhaps the key. Neither was hunting as successful without an accomplice. At Elmore Fiducia loved running free in our nine-acre garden. About the second day of her being with us I took the two deerhounds down on to our lower meadows at the back of the house. Fiducia was delighted with her new life and after saying hello to a herd of milking cows across the fence, she put up a hare – which secured her future acceptance! Zamara, having almost ignored her until now, suddenly saw her in a new light!

For the next seven years Fiducia, who I now called Ducci – a name she took to instantly – lived happily with Zamara, sharing their lives together at Elmore and enjoying daily walks on our 1,200 acres of land – including riverside walks on the banks of the Severn and occasionally watching the Severn Bore. Ducci lived until she was nearly ten. Everyone loved her and she loved everyone. She was a wonderful addition to our lives, and rescuing her was one of the most rewarding things I ever did in my life. She never stopped being grateful.

During this time I took Zamara to a number of stud dogs to be mated, as she had always yearned for puppies. But because it had not then become the rule for vets to have facilities for blood testing to pinpoint the exact date of ovulation – and she was always late in ovulating – we had for several years failed to achieve a mating. At last, at the age of seven-and-a-half and with the help of blood testing, success was achieved, and just three months short of her eighth birthday (which at that time the Kennel Club allowed) Zamara gave birth to eight

healthy puppies, three dogs and five bitches, all born naturally. Joyce Bond came to stay to be with us and help guide the first into this world. Zamara was the most wonderful and devoted mother and basked in the glory of motherhood. She was the proudest mother in the world! What a wonderful experience it was for all of us watching them grow up and enjoy an idyllic life as a pack spending their puppyhood days in the walled garden – where as they grew they chased and frequently caught ducks and pheasants who unwisely landed too close. What fun they had!

Because they were both conceived and born at the time of the camellias flowering, the puppies were all named after them, and for the following eight-and-a-half years I collected those camellias after which I had named the hounds. They are now a wonderful sight.

When registering the puppies with the Kennel Club I chose SAINTVALERY as my prefix. I did so because the Guise (de Gyse) family had originally come from Saint Valery in Normandy and it seemed

Below & opposite: Zamara keeps a watchful eye on her puppies.

appropriate to go back to our roots.

I kept four from the litter – and four went out into the world to families with whom I kept in touch throughout the lives of the hounds. I sent regular news of what the family at home was doing, with photographs to illustrate this. I also reported what they were being fed; this has always been entirely natural, following, as I have always done, the advice of Juliette de Bairacli Levy in her book *The Complete Herbal Handbook for the Dog and Cat.*

In 2003, when the young hounds were eleven months old, the Deerhound Club Breed Show was held near Cheltenham, a mere twenty minutes' drive from Elmore. I had not thought of showing them, as Zamara hadn't enjoyed the show ring, and it never occurred to me that her offspring would either. However, as so many people had tried to help me to achieve the litter, I felt that I wanted to show them, and so we finally made it. I entered them all (the four I had kept) and I also encouraged two others who had young hounds from the litter to enter them too.

As they were all the same age I had to enlist friends to help me show mine. Bjorn Kruger – a Deerhound Club member from Germany – was one who kindly helped me. The young hounds were only eleven months old at the time, so the Puppy Classes suited them well and they all had great success. We returned home with eight rosettes and I went back in the evening to join in the rest of the day's activities and collect two extremely handsome trophies: The Manshay Trophy, which Anticipation won for the Best Special Beginner, having won the Best Special Beginner Novice Bitch; and the Marjorie Bell Trophy, which Dazzler won for the Best Opposite Sex having won the Best Special Beginners Novice Dog. What a wonderful day we had had! . . . and what a debut!

Apart from being utterly exhausted and sleeping for practically the whole of the following day the young hounds had thoroughly enjoyed the occasion and the socialising.

We had been well schooled on the lawn at home over the preceding weeks by a friend who had for many years bred and shown another breed, and this was a huge help, not only for the hounds but also for me. Joyce Bond also came and gave us some schooling.

From then on I decided I would take them to more shows – but two at a time so that I could largely show them myself. Although on occasions when I had unavoidably entered two bitches in the same class both John Francis and Jenny Grimshaw – members of the Deerhound Club – helped me by showing one. The young hounds looked on these outings as huge treats. Bob Smith, who lives in the village, agreed to drive us to our various destinations and to sit on the bench with one of the hounds while I was in the ring with another. He invariably fell asleep but he had the lead in his fingers and would have known if his charge had wandered off! Over the years we all had a massive amount of fun and did remarkably well. Some of the outings we went on I took all the young hounds. These were chiefly to the Breed Shows, when we travelled in Bob's transit van which he divided up inside like a horsebox; this gave the young hounds individual space and they always travelled in the same compartment. They enjoyed these outings so much that they used to start 'singing' when Bob would have been leaving home – a good ten minutes before he arrived. Then they greeted him with enormous enthusiasm and leapt into the van before even the bedding or anything else had been put on board! To them it didn't matter where we were going – we were going somewhere. That was all that mattered! As far as showing was concerned I don't think they particularly loved the show ring – apart from Hope and Dazzler, who became very aware of the judge's view on the day. Undoubtedly they both loved doing well. At that time, the day usually finished up on a more lighthearted note. This was the Brace, when we were asked to go round the ring with two hounds and they were judged on their similarity and performance. Hope and Dream Girl (known at home as Hopes and Dreams) were similar in height and size and went round the ring at speed and in complete unison. Bob, looking on from the ringside said they simply travelled as one. They did extremely well at this and they knew they were good

Zamara awaits the arrival of Father Christmas on the Oak Room bed at Elmore.

at it. They loved it!

When the young hounds were merely weeks old a family called Allen moved into the village. Nick and Debbie had two small children – a son Tom and his younger sister Kate who was seven. Kate was brought by her mother to see the puppies and was completely entranced by them! From then on Debbie would bring her to the house and leave her for a while before returning to collect her. Over the ensuing years Kate came and played with the young hounds, helped teach them to go on the lead, and enjoyed taking them for walks with me. She seldom had suitable clothes for the weather and invariably ended up in some of mine – which to her seemed all part of the fun!

Eventually she had some lessons in showing from John Francis and thereafter, whenever school permitted, came with us – and more latterly helped to show them. She did extremely well at this as she is quite competitive and this all helped!

Kate lead training . . . sometimes it was more successful than others.

Kate more suitably dressed!

7 (continued).
Capture the Spirit

These are the profiles that encapsulate the spirit of each of the four young hounds throughout their lives and adventures . . .

SAINTVALERY ANTICIPATION

I think that Anticipation was probably the pick of the litter, and the pick of the four that I kept – although it would have been a close-run thing. All of them did extremely well in the show ring. Paishi, as she was known at home, was passionate about everything she did. She had from the very beginning been deeply attached to me – as if she was destined in some way to be my protector. Her companion was her litter brother Dazzler, and between them they became formidable hunters. Paishi found the quarry and Dazzler was wherever he was needed to hunt it. Foxes and hares were their quarry. Sometimes when exercising them I had difficulty in knowing where they were, as with our own land they had wonderful free-running exercise. It was as if they had some secret message between themselves that seemed to say: 'From now on you can't hear her, right!' and off they'd go – sometimes not to be seen for some considerable time. For a while I had to separate them and take each of them out with an older dog, in order to be confident that I would bring them back!

Eventually I was able to take them out together once more – which, of course, they loved.

Paishi was a beautiful bitch and moved like a dancer. However, she was not so keen on the show ring as she felt it was of limited interest and a pretty poor second to hunting. However, she was always happy to please me – whatever it took.

Over the following years I took the hounds to most of the shows that were within a reasonable distance from home. We did remarkably well and had an enormous amount of fun. As they were all the same age I had to divide their outings between them so none of them went very frequently – but they enjoyed it when they did. In 2005 we had a particularly enjoyable Breed Show weekend – we won the Breeder's Group, having been joined by another of their litter who lived in Cornwall. The judge said that they looked as alike as peas in a pod!

Photos: Carol Ann Johnson

SAINTVALERY DAZZLER

Dazzler was a charming dog – a real character and such a happy chap. He loved people and when friends came to the house he always gave them such a very warm welcome. I think he thought that they had come primarily to see him! He was a great communicator – and he had a wonderful smile. He had high self-esteem, and being prepared for an event, or generally being groomed and tidied up, suited his vanity. He was very straightforward, and you could read his mind clearly! Taking after his mother Zamara, he liked to make his own decisions – but he didn't always get away with it! He had a great sense of fun. He had presence in a very charming way, and perfect old-fashioned manners.

Ever since he was a young hound he had something about him that made me feel he was an 'old soul' and perhaps had been here before. He was thoughtful and very wise – way beyond his years. When young he had been nervous of the show ring, although when he eventually found that he had become less nervous and more confident, he thought he'd show off instead! I found that he was too strong for me in the show ring in those early days and enlisted the help of a male friend. But when I decided to pick up the reins myself I much enjoyed showing him. He was always aware when he had done well, and was crestfallen when he was overlooked. But the outing always gave him great pleasure.

Dazzler enjoying a day's lure coursing in Salisbury 2005.

At the Tudor hunting lodge at Lodge Park. Kate Allen with Dream Girl and Hope, Bob Smith with Dazzler and Sally with Anticipation - all suitably dressed!

SAINTVALERY HOPE

Gentle and loving – and hugely appealing – Saintvalery Hope gave me endless love and pleasure. Her companion was litter sister Dream Girl and at home they were known as Hopes and Dreams. Hope loved life in every aspect and was always full of fun. Her spirit remained young throughout her entire life – right to the end. She also loved the show ring, and always knew when she had done well.

A memorable day for me was when Hope won the Reserve Challenge Certificate to Dream Girl's Challenge Certificate at Richmond Championship Show in the summer of 2005. Angela Randell was the judge that day – and there was a heartwarming show of support from the ringside as she made her choice. Later she wrote a glowing critique. Hope and Dream Girl also loved doing the Brace at the end of the day and if they were asked to move, as they generally were, they were in total unison – completely synchronized. How they enjoyed it! They knew they were good!

Hope had an eternally youthful outlook on life and as a young hound had a particularly flippant

attitude to discipline! However, throughout her entire life, she never did anything wrong, or said a cross word. She had a completely flawless character but a great sense of fun, and like Dazzler a wonderful smile.

(Left to Right) Hope, Dream Girl, Anticipation and Dazzler.

photo john wiggon

SAINTVALERY DREAM GIRL

The smallest of the litter but with great personality, Dream Girl went on to become the alpha bitch. She had subtle but supreme self-confidence. Dreams had charm and adored attention. Like her litter brother Dazzler she was a great communicator and had a very engaging smile! She was interested in everything and everyone – a real busybody! She was a comedienne – the Court jester – full of fun and original ideas; for example, if she thought she hadn't been noticed she would sometimes appear unexpectedly at eye level to make sure that she was! Another ploy was that, if she thought that she would like to lie where one of the others was sleeping, she would simply go and lie on top of them until they decided that the best plan was to move. It worked like a charm! She had humour and mischief! When she knew that she was being mischievous she gently wagged her tail . . . and grinned!

In the show ring her size was not in her favour, but she had beautiful conformation – and moved like a dream. She did not go unnoticed and early in her career won Limit Bitch, Reserve Best of Breed, and Best Opposite Sex at the South West Hound Show in the spring of 2005. Clare Churchill was the judge that day. It was later that year at Richmond Championship Show that she won the Bitch Challenge Certificate from Limit Bitch – with Hope winning the Reserve Challenge Certificate. Dreams went on to win the Reserve Best of Breed. Angela Randall was the judge that day. It was a very special day.

THE DEERHOUND CLUB

OPEN SINGLE BREED SHOW
Saturday, 18th & Sunday, 19th APRIL 2009

F I R S T

Class No. ....

Exhibit ....

Judges
Saturday: M............................
Su....................
Dun...................

Left: Hope
Right: Dream Girl

bjphotography

Left: Hope   Right: Dream Girl.

Saintvalery Hounds, winners of the Special Breeder's Group, 2007 Deerhound Breed Show - Dazzler, Dream Girl, Anticipation, Hope & Donation.

Dazzler, Dream Girl and Hope in the capable hands of Bob Smith.

Back to their Roots

One year, as I made my plans to go north to the Scottish Breed Show, which is held near Edinburgh in March, I thought that it would be a good opportunity to go to Ardno where some great friends of mine had moved. The husband had previously been gamekeeper to our family shoot at Elmore, and his wife had been a great help in the house at such times as the Cheltenham Festival Meeting, for which my husband John had a large house party and the house was full to bursting!

So this is what I did. Ardno is very close to Ardkinglas, the seat of the Noble family, and my friends knew the Noble family well. So while we were staying with them we took a drive to the church where Anastasia Noble was buried as I wanted to visit her grave. As it happened, we arrived at the church just as the vicar and his organist were coming out after morning service, and we chatted. I told the vicar that I was making a pilgrimage and I asked him if he had officiated at Miss Noble's funeral. He told me that although another priest had done so he had been there. I went on to search for the grave which in such a small place was not hard to find.

As my hounds are descended from Ardkinglas hounds on both sides of their pedigree, this was indeed an important and sentimental pilgrimage, and the bonus was to find that at the time of my visit there were two camellias in the small churchyard that were both in bloom. Camellias, as I have already explained, featured importantly in our lives. Having had an imaginary chat with Miss Noble at her grave we went on to look at Ardkinglas House and I met David Sumption who now lives there with his young wife and family.

Not infrequently since I've had my hounds I've found myself wondering what Miss Noble would have done in various predicaments that I have been faced with and something has told me what that might be. She was the most remarkable person, with very pronounced views and, of course, huge experience of deerhounds. I feel extremely fortunate to have known her albeit only towards the end of her life, and I like to think when I have had a query that she is somehow able to advise me from her heavenly place.

I can remember clearly when I was showing my three dog hound puppies to a prospective new home that I felt a very firm influence telling me to 'Take Dazzler out of this'. This continued until I told the people who were with me that after all I was going to take Dazzler out of the picture.

On another occasion I was having trouble in knowing where Paishi and Dazzler were when I took them out exercising and they disappeared. I asked myself what would miss Noble have done in a similar situation. I imagined that she would have taken an older hound out with one of the young ones – one at a time. This proved to be the answer.

One year I won in a Breed Show raffle, a small silver dog collar which had been part of Miss Noble's estate and left to the Deerhound Club. It is inscribed with the words 'Miss Bailey', which must have been the name of a beloved pet.

This collar I keep perched on the corner of a picture of Miss Noble by Mick Cawston which hangs in my hall. One day the collar suddenly fell off the picture and hurtled across the hall. I felt as if Miss Noble was telling me firmly to get on and mate my bitch!

All these things have been such good advice... and so firmly given!

Above: Miss Nobel's grave at Kilmorich Church.
Below: Ardkinglas House.

Alternatives . . .
Medicines and Therapies

I have always been a believer in alternatives – whether it be medicine, communication or healing.

I first came across homeopathy when I read a very interesting article in a newspaper about a vet who had turned to homeopathy when he decided he was tired of treating animals with chemicals. Shortly afterwards my deerhound bitch Zamara developed a bladder stone. My vet at the time had suggested there were two possible ways of dealing with this. The first would be to try her on a particular diet. When we tried this Zamara was constantly hungry and used to wake me up in the night so that she could go outside and forage under the copper beech tree in the garden to see if there were any remains from the fox having eaten its supper.

Having tried the first suggestion without success as it didn't cure the problem, the vet then suggested the only other option that he knew about would be an operation. I asked the vet whether, before we resorted to an operation, he would mind if I contacted the homeopathic vet I had read about – to which he happily agreed. I telephoned Richard Allport and told him about the problem that my deerhound bitch was having, and asked him if he had come across this situation before, and whether he thought he could help. Yes, he told me. He had come across this before – and in a deerhound. So I took Zamara to see him. He cured her completely within five weeks and my vet was completely astonished.

Some years before I had been given a copy of Juliette de Bairacli Levy's book *The Complete Herbal Handbook for the Dog and Cat*. Juliette's philosophy prescribes the use of everything completely natural, from food to cures, and in her book she says that a contributing factor to the cause of a bladder stone is chlorinated tap water. I immediately switched Zamara's food to raw everything – meat, fish, fruit and vegetables. I also thereafter gave her bottled water, although latterly when I had more hounds I gave them filtered water; but always raw everything in their feed. She thrived on this and so have the remaining hounds.

ANIMAL COMMUNICATION

When Zamara's puppies were a few months old I wanted to introduce them one at a time to Ducci. I decided one day to bring Paishi out into the garden and let Ducci meet her. At first Ducci was very friendly towards Paishi and played with her a little, before getting her down and firmly standing over her. I was very alarmed and wondered what she was going to do to her. She made no noise and was not cross with Paishi, but was decidedly making her point. I stepped in and suggested that perhaps this wasn't such a good idea after all.

I then wondered whose help I could turn to and came up with the idea of an animal communicator. I was given the name and contact number of such a person, Elaine Downs of Animal Matters in Lancashire. I contacted her and told her my problem, asking if she felt she could help. She agreed and communicated with Ducci, who told her that Paishi was a little upstart and that she needed putting in her place. She had no intention of hurting her but merely teaching her a lesson. As far as pecking order went Ducci obviously felt she was higher and that Paishi had to learn this. There was no doubt that she did!

Some time later when Paishi and Dazzler used

to disappear for such long periods of time when out on a walk, I had to seriously think about what to do. Again I got in touch with Elaine and told her the problem. She said she would talk to Paishi which she subsequently did.

As I have said, I thought Miss Noble would probably have taken an older hound out with a young one and the older hound would with luck bring it back. I tried this, knowing that Ducci was jealous. I looked into her face and told her I wanted her help. I had a problem that Paishi was away too long going hunting on a walk. I asked Ducci to try and prevent this happening. I might add Ducci herself was a keen huntress – but it was worth a try! I took the two of them up the fields on leads and then let them off. Paishi soon realised with delight that she was free (something I had not allowed her for some time while I worked out a solution to my problem). She immediately headed down toward the field at the bottom of the hill. Amazingly, Ducci tried to cut her off three times, but Paishi skipped sideways and onwards. Ducci then decided to stay with her and down to the bottom of the hill they went and into the field below, where there were usually hares about. Although Ducci was a keen huntress she had a responsibility to me that day and she knew it. I watched them hunt their way through this field for a while – eventually they returned to me together much to my relief and surprise. When they got back to where I was standing waiting and watching I made a great fuss of them both. I told Ducci that she was such a clever girl and that she was so good. She licked Paishi's face and was delighted that I was so pleased with her. She was never jealous again and we had a completely happy household.

How extremely interesting all these things have been to learn.

SPIRITUAL HEALING

This is another form of help I have turned to and came across Helen the Healer though Richard Allport, in whose Clinic she has a room and from where she works from time to time. Helen, too, has enormous ability to identify a problem – and from a distance when necessary. On a number of occasions I have asked her to help diagnose a symptom – and she has been absolutely spot on – often saving me a huge amount of anxiety and expense.

Helen is also able to calm animals in a traumatic situation – again if necessary from a distance. How lucky I have been to come across such wonderful help.

McTIMONEY CHIROPRACTIC THERAPY

This is another form of alternative help I have turned to. Currently I seek help from Paula Fisher-Stokes who practices from Worcestershire, but she is happy to travel and visit people to treat their animals. She is one of the most highly respected practitioners in her field, and takes a room near the N.E.C. during Crufts, where she treats animals who come to her from all over the world. McTimoney is a form of chiropractic therapy and is both highly effective and non- traumatic for the animals.

As deerhounds are very athletic and at Elmore had a great deal of free running exercise, I felt that it was important to have them regularly checked over about every six months – just to keep their limbs in good order. This proved to be a good idea and I think probably saved them a lot of trouble in later years. The speed at which they run means that they can so easily hurt themselves or each other.

I do think that I have been enormously lucky to have been able to turn to such excellent forms of help. I have also been extremely fortunate in having excellent vets.

8.

The End of an Era

Gradually during 2005 John's strength began to diminish. He ceased to wish to take part in things that had previously given him great pleasure. He told his friends that he would no longer be able to host his much-loved house party for the Cheltenham Festival Meeting. Eventually he slipped quietly into the next world. During this time Harry Dalzell Payne, who had a flat in the house, was very kind, and supportive.

John's funeral was another wonderful example of everyone pulling together. His tenant farmers were his pall bearers and, following a very moving funeral service, a huge number of wonderful friends all sang the hymns that we had chosen for our wedding. It was impossible for them all – including many members of the Jockey Club, the Deerhound Club,

the entire village community of Elmore and our much loved postman – to fit into our (not so small) village church. However, speakers had been set up for those who were outside – together with chairs. It was a wonderful 'send off'.

John is buried in the family plot in the churchyard. Grown men cried at the wake in the garden at Elmore afterwards. Magically, in the middle of what had been a spell of wet weather the sun shone and the garden looked at its best. May is, in my view, one of the most beautiful months of the year. It was 23rd May, 2007.

John's long-time friend Harry Dalzell Payne, who had been such a great friend, particularly over the previous thirty years since he had had a flat at Elmore, gave this eulogy:

A TRIBUTE TO SIR JOHN GUISE, BART., OF ELMORE COURT 1927-2007
by Harry Dalzell Payne - 23rd MAY, 2007

On the South wall of Gloucester Cathedral there is a memorial which reads in part: 'His excellent disposition, conciliatory manner, judgement, good sense and principles of unsullied honour, gave him an ascendancy among his peers. His hospitality was splendid without profusion. His friendship was active without profession. His munificence extensive without pretension'.

That memorial is to the honour and memory of the Sir John Guise who lived from 1734 to 1794 and the words used there could not be more appropriate in recognising the rare qualities of our friend Sir John Guise we are met together today to honour. I like to think that it is also proof positive of the truth and value of the hereditary principle. The Guises always have been and always will be good people, and John was one of the best.

Son of Sir Anselm and Lady Margaret Guise, John was born in 1927. He already had an elder sister Philippa and later a younger brother Jamie and they made a very happy family. The children spent an idyllic childhood at Elmore before the Second World War came, when the family moved to Scotland while the house was requisitioned for the duration of the War. John went to school at Winchester and showed early signs of his acute intelligence and dry wit. He then went to Sandhurst and joined the Third King's Own Hussars and served as a regular Officer for the next sixteen years. He was always mindful of his forebear Captain J.G. Guise, later Lieutenant General, whose Memorial is on the church wall to the right of the altar here, and won one of the first VCs – at Lucknow in the Indian Mutiny in 1857. There were so many deeds of outstanding bravery in his Regiment at that time but only one of them could be recognised and he was voted by his brother Officers 'the bravest of the brave' and awarded the medal.

Sir John's time in the Army was a very happy one. He made a host of friends- not only in his own Regiment but throughout the Cavalry. He made a name for himself in amateur steeplechases in Germany, besides being an efficient and popular Officer. He was noted Adjutant of his Regiment and virtually ran it for a time under a weak Commanding Officer. In 1957 his Regiment was amalgamated with the 7th Queen's Own Hussars of which I was a member.

He soldiered on for a few more years but the amalgamation was not to his liking and he eventually resigned his commission saying – I hope with his tongue in his cheek – 'I couldn't possibly go on serving in the same Regiment as that ambitious fellow Dalzell Payne'. We had met for the first time at Sandhurst in 1948.

For a time after leaving the Army he farmed a herd of cows with willing weekend help from various friends, and then served as a Starter with the Jockey Club for the next twenty-four years, motoring over forty thousand miles annually and starting races at every racecourse in Britain. His punctuality was a feature of his life and his association with the jockeys and racing officials was firm, humorous and much respected. For many years before and after his retirement as a Starter he hosted the annual meeting of the Racing Officials Association at Elmore. And it's good to see them so well represented here today. He would have appreciated that.

Having succeeded Sir Anselm in 1970, he assumed his responsibilities at Elmore and showed himself to be a worthy senior trustee of the family estate for the next thirty-seven years, generous to a degree, mindful of the difficulties of others and always aware of his responsibilities to keep the Estate intact for his heirs and assigns. All this with the expert help of his factor, first Francis and then his son John Penley. Examples of his devotion to the interests of his tenants spring to mind in his compassionate reaction to the foot and mouth outbreak of 2001. And he was always a great friend to all in the Sporting world, particularly to the country folk of the Berkeley Vale. He was indeed one of 'the old school' sharing great respect and friendship with like-minded folk of any station in life.

1992 was a special year in his life – and the life of the village – when he married Sally Stevens, virtually the girl next door from Frampton. John's choice of spouse was a hallmark of his good sense and good luck. Sally brought into his life companionship, love, a youthful and modernising element to Elmore Court and a desire to help the village in every way she thought appropriate. She also bred at Elmore a pack of wonderful prize winning Scottish deerhounds, don't I know it! – I live just above them.

Elmore Court has always been a particularly happy place, with a warm welcome for all and sundry, even more so when Sally arrived. There was the occasional Hunt Ball and frequent fund raising events for good causes, displays on the lawn, conducted tours of the house for interested parties, the annual Lawn Meet of the Berkeley Hunt and family Christmases and the Christmas village lunches and children's parties were always such good fun because they were meticulously organised. Then Jamie started up the shoot again with the help of Michael and Jennifer Watts and for the last twenty years increasingly good sport has been shown. But for John and his racing friends the annual Cheltenham National Hunt Festival was a highlight of the Elmore year. Each March for more than thirty years up to twenty friends would assemble at Elmore for the three –now four days' racing. Invitations were on a dead man's shoes basis and it soon became one of the most exclusive clubs in England with wonderful and endless hospitality reminiscent of a bye gone age. I guess most of the members of that exclusive club are here today, the senior members being John's very good friends Dan and Sue Abbott.

Another of John's contributions was to the Turf Club in London where he was Chairman for three years from 1983-1986 and greatly expanded the membership among the racing fraternity. His natural discretion always prevented him from retelling some of the more scandalous events of those times, but the Turf Club and particularly its staff had a special place in his affections. And it's good to see The Turf Club represented here today – again, he would have very much appreciated that.

And so now the baton passes to Jamie and Carole, now Sir James and Lady Guise – and their children Anselm and Ruthie. We wish them all the very best of good fortune in their new responsibilities, particularly Anselm. And of course there will be changes in due course – but Elmore is somewhat averse to Change. I am reminded of John and Sally's wedding reception for the tenants of the Estate, John had persuaded Sally to say a few words which she did most graciously. And as they left the dais in hall at Elmore, John tuned and said to everyone 'Mind you, there won't be any changes at Elmore'. Voice from the back – 'Changes, there haven't been any changes at Elmore for 800 years'.

Finally we thank all those who cared for Sir John at the end, especially the nurses and his devoted staff Bronia and Rex from St. Helena who served him so loyally for more than five years. And so we join his grieving family Sally, Philippa, her children and grandchildren, Jamie, Carole and their children in saying good bye to John Guise. To them and to Elmore we wish, as John would, all the very best for the future. Thanks be to God for John, such a kind friend, amusing companion, wise counsellor and generous host and landowner. May God rest his soul in peace.

Leightons Farmhouse.

A few months after John had left us and gone to Heaven, the hounds and I went to live in Leightons a charming sixteenth-century farmhouse on the estate, where we settled in very happily to pick up our lives again and to pursue some of our dreams.

Anselm Guise, John's nephew, inherited Elmore

and moved into the house for a while before turning it into a very successful venue for weddings.

It was an enormous privilege for me to be a part of the family history . . . and also a very great pleasure.

GOD BLESS ELMORE

Postscript

In our farmhouse Paishi and Dazzler slept upstairs with me – Paishi sleeping on my bed and Dazzler on the floor beside us. When we arrived I could hear rats in the loft above my bedroom, and I found this extremely frightening, so I brought the hounds up to protect me! Then I had the rats dealt with! However, being country property in the middle of a farming community, it is an ongoing problem.

Over the years I did a considerable amount of restoration work generally adapting the house and outbuildings to our various needs. This too became a much-loved home where we received our family and friends – sometimes with their deerhounds.

I continued to take the hounds to shows, both Championship Shows and Deerhound Club Breed Shows, all of which we enjoyed enormously. We all did! I am lucky enough to have done most of my showing when one could expect an entry of at least 100-150 in the breed at a Championship Show so success was very rewarding.

SAINTVALERY ANTICIPATION

On one occasion when Paishi had won Best of Breed at Midland Counties Championship Show in October, 2007 – having won the Open Bitch class – under Brenda Jarrett who was the judge that day – she went on to the Hound Group. Paishi seemed to tell me that she had already done a great deal for me that day and wasn't it time to go home!

I believed that Paishi had been carrying puppies at the time when John was losing his fight for life, and that she subsequently lost them. It was a particularly desperate time for all of us. Later I tried to put her in whelp again – several times – but somehow we never achieved it. I think this saddened her a great deal. However, she had an otherwise extremely happy life and plenty of interest and variety, and knew only too well how much she was loved. She lived until she was nearly thirteen and is buried among the camellia trees in my orchard, along with her brother, Dazzler, and two sisters, Hope and Dream Girl.

SAINTVALERY HOPE

At the age of seven and a half Hope gave birth to a single puppy, Saintvalery Inspiration (Nell). Hope proved to be a wonderful mother and right to the end of her life continued her motherly role of tidying up her daughter. She lived until she was eleven and died as the result of having a collapsed larynx. Although this was diagnosed immediately and she was given a temporary operation, her condition deteriorated and I took the very hard decision of letting her go to Heaven. Oh! how I missed her. They say 'It is better to have loved and lost than never to have loved at all'. How true.

SAINTVALERY DAZZLER

Dazzler lived until he was ten and a half. He had begun to lose the strength in his back legs, which meant that he had to cut back on some of his activities. This irritated him to start with but he came to terms with it, and learned to live quite contentedly within his limitations. He was still able to trot up our large field each day and insisted on galloping back down again – albeit rather precariously. It was therefore a massive shock to come down one morning and find he had gone to Heaven. How does one come to terms with this? What a massive hole he left in our hearts and in our lives.

I comforted myself that he had had a marvellous life, with lots of interest and variety and plenty of free-running exercise. He knew only too well how much he was loved, and I hope he knows now how much he is missed. God bless you Dazzler. You made this world a better place. You are with me everywhere. I will never forget you.

SAINTVALERY DREAM GIRL

Dream Girl lived until she was over twelve. One of her great joys was helping in the garden. Whatever I was doing she liked to join in and she never left me until I had finished. Toward the end of her life she slipped on the kitchen floor and did the splits. I tried a wide variety of remedies: McTimoney, deep heat, massage, pain killers and also spiritual healing, but somehow we could not override the damage. It was pitiful to see how she struggled to cope. She was so brave. Finally I decided that she had put up with enough and I asked the vet to come to the house and help her to Heaven. What a huge hole she left in our hearts and in our lives. She was so bossy! She was always the voice of the group, and if anyone had something to say she raised her voice above the others to make sure I had heard . . . and did something about it! The house seemed so empty without her. We all struggled to cope. I never could have imagined how deeply it would affect the others, each of them reacting in their own way. God Bless you Dream Girl – you gave us so much love and pleasure while you were with us. Your humour and originality were so refreshing. You were an amazing role model for us all and we will try our best to live up to the standards you have set. Watch over us from your Heavenly place . . . and don't ever leave us. We will never forget you.

How do any of us come to terms with losing one of our beloved deerhounds? As with the others when their time came, I tried to comfort myself that they had all had wonderful, happy and interesting lives with lots of variety, and have known only too well how much they were loved.

It is their wonderful spirit that moves me most: their unmatchable standards of loyalty and devotion; their amazing ability to accept what life brings – and simply rise above it. What an example they are to us all!

In my view they are in a league of their own and we who are lucky enough to share life with them are truly fortunate. They give us such an amazing variety of experiences. They leave us with the most wonderful memories and are catalysts for making lifelong friends. Each one of them implants an indelible print on our hearts that time will never erase.

My hounds are generally known as the old-fashioned type – unusual to find these days but entirely appropriate to me being part of a very old family and living in a house steeped in history. It was partly this that led me to choose deerhounds as companions when I got married – deerhounds being one of the oldest breed of hunting hounds. With our land and with plenty of space it all seemed so natural. What a wonderful part of my life they have been – and continue to be. How blessed I am.

SAINTVALERY INSPIRATION

Nell became Sally's sole companion, a role she flourished in and she was a tremdous support and comfort to Sally throughout her illness. Nell is now adapting to a different life with a family in Sussex.

Lightning Source UK Ltd.
Milton Keynes UK
UKOW07n1208210717

305629UK00007B/15/P